People of Passion

Activities
for Opening Doors
to Your Community

For more information, please contact
Transforming Churches Network
1160 Vickery Ln. Ste #1, Cordova, TN 38016
901-757-9700
www.transformingchurchesnetwork.org
terry@transformingchurchesnetwork.org

Table of Contents

Introduction

Who are People of Passion? Obviously, passion comes from something that you feel strongly about. In the context of churches reaching their community with the Gospel of Jesus Christ, passion is needed in three areas:

1. Passion for Christ: If you love Jesus and want others to know Him and love Him the way you do, then you could be a Person of Passion.
2. Passion for your Church: If you love your local congregation and have a deep desire for your church to be everything that God wants it to be, then you could be a Person of Passion.
3. Passion for your Community: If you care about people in your community, especially those who don't know Jesus and His love for them, then you could be a Person of Passion.

Notice that you don't have to be a Person of Position. You don't have to be a Board Member or an elected official or a leader of any kind; just someone who is willing to step out and learn. In fact, in some ways, it will be beneficial for you if you are not currently serving in some official capacity at your church. Why? Not because People of Position can't also be People of Passion. It's just that if you don't have any official responsibilities (and don't have to be attending other meetings), you will have a lot more time, energy, and yes, PASSION, for the kind of missional activities suggested in this booklet.

What do People of Passion do? Very simply put, they join together in activities that will help their church open doors for the Gospel into their local community. To be clear, Jesus is the only door into heaven and into the church (John 10:9a). We receive salvation by grace alone through faith in Him (Ephesians 2:8-9). And yet, while there is only one way into the church, there are many doors that lead back out to the community where large groups of lost people can still be found.

So People of Passion are kind of like hinges! They help their church discover creative ways to open new doors into their communities. Without hinges, church doors are nothing more than walls. Equipped with hinges, however, the doors of the church can swing open to unlimited opportunities for reaching lost people with the Gospel.

This booklet is a collection of door-opening activities. They are designed for a small group of approximately seven people to work together and implement. (Small churches may have less than seven and if your group size exceeds ten, simply start a second group!) They are not focused primarily on Bible study or content discussion. They are action-oriented guides that will give you exposure to new ways of being God's people. Each activity will feature a new outreach idea and discussion guide for carrying out that activity. In short, these are to be Bible doin' groups! "But be doers of the word, and not hearers only..." (James 1:22).

Finally, each group should have a facilitator. The facilitator is NOT a teacher. These are not meetings where a leader will be called upon to provide tons of information or to preach. This is not to say that the pastor or another staff person cannot or should not convene the group. Rather, the facilitator's main function in this group experience is to help the participants share what they are learning together, to prepare for the upcoming outreach initiative or homework, and to ensure that all plans are carried out. People learn best when they are able to share their experiences with their peers and are given the freedom to enter into dialogue around those experiences. That was Jesus' methodology with His first disciples, and it still works great today.

Ultimately, it is our hope and prayer that the activities in this booklet will translate into a passion for the lost. Having experienced the grace and love of God through Christ in our own lives, we know that sharing this Good News with others can be one of the highlights of our walk with Jesus. May God teach you in new and surprising ways as you join together with other People of Passion in opening doors for the Gospel in your community!

Key Questions

1. What is the timetable for completing these activities?

   Most groups will want to take approximately 6 months (See Timeline, p. 9).

   This gives ample time for homework, practice, and research between sessions. Another option is to meet every week and complete the process in 12-14 weeks. If the shorter option is used, some activities will likely need to be skipped and/or done between sessions.

2. Do they all need to be done in order?

   The activities are set up in such a way that they build upon each other. For example, the Prayer Walking and Community Surveying modules provide needed research to complete the Visioning Day. In turn, crafting a Vision Statement, with an identifiable target and well-defined strategy will inform what kind of Service Projects and Outreach Events would be the most effective in engaging your community.

3. What do we do with the Prayerwalking Game Plan after it is developed?

   Use it! At the beginning of every session, it would be helpful to spend a few minutes asking everyone what they have learned from the previous session(s) and how they are implementing this new learning, i.e., take time to hold each other accountable for exercising door-opening activities individually and as a group!

4. Is it possible to write out the church's vision in one day/session?

   It is possible, if all the homework and preparation—Community Interviews & Surveys, Demographics, etc.—has been done in advance. In most cases, it will take several sessions if the People of Passion group does this work. The Pastor and/or Staff, along with another small group, could be an effective option for need to completing this task.

5. Are there other resources available to supplement this booklet?

   Yes, go to our website, www.transformingchurchesnetwork.org and click on People of Passion.

6. What do we do when we finish these activities?

There are several options:

- You can start over with another group.

- You can ask each person to recruit a new group and be the facilitator for that new group. This would give you multiple groups and make the most impact on your church and community!

- You can repeat the process with the same group.

- Combine these ideas, or come up with your own!

7. Do we need to repeat every module in the future?

Not necessarily. If you are happy with your Vision Statement and believe that you have a good handle on the needs of your community, you may want to skip the Community Survey and Vision Day modules the next time around. However, repeating those activities with new people will go far toward helping them to gain ownership of the vision and to open their eyes to what God is doing in the community.

Timeline and Overview

Unit	Subject	Overview	Time Needed
1.	Prayerwalking	Gaining practical experience in praying for a community and for those who need Christ.	2 weeks
2.	Community Surveying	Uncovering the real needs of a community by interacting with community leaders in the area or city.	4-6 weeks
3.	Visioning Day	Crafting a compelling Vision Statement that identifies your mission target and outlines a simple strategy for reaching that target.	4-6 weeks
4.	Service Projects	Choosing a service project that the group will practice as a tangible blessing to the community.	4 weeks
5.	Personal Testimony	Building a story that can be shared in less than five minutes which highlights how God has worked in your life.	2 weeks
6.	Outreach Events	Planning and executing an outreach event for the church that will include volunteer recruitment and event promotion.	4 weeks
7.	Gospel Presentation	Learning and practicing a simple method for sharing the Gospel with a friend or stranger.	2 weeks

Preparation List

1. Prayerwalking
- "Prayerwalking Your Community" DVD or Internet Connection

2. Community Surveying
- None needed

3. Visioning Day
- Whiteboard or Flipchart or Computer & Projector
- "Sister Act" DVD

4. Service Projects
- Whiteboard or Flipchart

5. Personal Testimony
- Paper
- Pens

6. Outreach Events
- Post-it-notes
- Whiteboard or Flipchart

7. Gospel Presentation
- Whiteboard or Flipchart
- Bibles
- Paper
- Pens

1   Prayer Walking

Introduction

Prayerwalking is simply praying while walking. That much is obvious. But there is more. Most of the time, we go about our busy lives, passing by houses, people, and businesses, focused on our daily tasks. Prayerwalking is a way to wake up to what is going on all around us. It is a way to see people, needs, and situations that call out for the touch of God. It is a way to attain God's heart for your local community and begin to pray that God might work in people and through you.

Below are five activities for getting involved with prayer walking. There are a few options for working through these activities. They include:

• Doing them all in one extended time. For instance, you could meet on Saturday morning and work through all five.
• Doing them over a series of two or three meetings. You could do Activities #1 and #2 in one meeting and then #3, #4, and #5 in a second.
• Choosing the activities that would work best for your team and do them. Feel free to adapt them to better fit your situation.

30-45
minutes

Activity #1: Take a Walk

Facilitator Instructions:
Instruct everyone that they have 10 minutes to go for a walk in groups of 2-3. As they walk, they are to pray for various needs in the community. They can pray silently or aloud as they walk whichever way they are most comfortable. Allow the following words that start with "P" to be their prayer guide.

- Pray for People
- Pray for Pain
- Pray for Problems
- Pray for Places

Debrief:
Once everyone is gathered back together, spend some time debriefing the experience with the following questions:

Question #1: What was the experience like for you?

Question #2: What are some possible benefits of praying while walking in a community?

Reflections:

Activity #2: Prayerwalking Video Clip

20 minutes

Facilitator Instructions:

Pick one of the options below ahead of time:

Option#1:

Go to the following YouTube website or find another by doing an internet search for prayerwalking videos and show a short clip for the group.

http://www.youtube.com/watch?v=4ugHZnTSK04

Option #2:

Pre-Order the DVD entitled "Prayerwalking Your Community" available from Church Leader Insights at www.churchleaderinsights.com or call 800-264-5124.

Before you view the video together, ask people to pay attention for one thing that really grabs their attention which they can share with the group after the video is completed. After the video is completed, share the personal highlights together.

Reflections:

15
minutes

Activity #3: Prayerwalking Article

Facilitator Instructions:
This activity works best if everyone reads the article (see pages 15-16) before gathering as a team. However, ask people if they need some time to review the article before discussing it. If so, then give them 10 minutes to work through the article. After everyone has the read the article, ask the group to respond to the following questions:

• What new ideas for praying in the community stood out to you from the article?

• What idea(s) would you like to incorporate into your prayerwalks in the future?

Reflections:

Prayerwalking Article

In hundreds of cities across the globe, ordinary believers are prayerwalking through the streets of their communities. They pray while walking, with eyes open for the spiritual awakening God is bringing. There is no set pattern or proven formula. Prayerwalkers have set out with every imaginable style. There's nothing magical about praying while walking. God's Spirit is simply helping us to pray in the midst of the very settings in which we expect Him to answer our prayers. We instinctively draw near to those for whom we pray. Getting up close to the community focuses our prayer. We sharpen our prayers by concentrating on specific homes and families. But we enlarge our praying as well, crying out for entire communities to know God's healing presence. Prayerwalks give us a simple way to fill the streets with prayer. Many are praying city-size prayers while ranging throughout their towns with disciplined regularity in small bands of two or three. In limited-access countries, thousands of "tourists" walk the streets interceding for the lost in their own communities. Thus prayerwalkers keep near the lost in order to touch them with the Gospel and transforming service. Quiet triumphs often follow as God changes the city day by day and house by house.

Getting Started: 7 Steps to Consider in Prayerwalking

1. **Join with other believers.** Join your faith with others to help prayer flow in an engaging conversation. Large groups sometimes fail to give everyone a chance to participate. Pairs and triplets work best. (For example, a group of eight could naturally divide into pairs as they walk, but be in sight of each other or meet back together at a certain location.)
2. **Set aside time.** Allowing one or two full hours gives prayerwalkers a good chance to manage preliminaries and follow-up discussions, although much can be done in less time.
3. **Choose an area.** Ask God to guide you. It's best by far to learn the joys of prayerwalking in unfamiliar neighborhoods. You'll return quickly to your own neighborhood with fresh vision. Centers of commerce and religion are fascinating, but there's nothing like touching families, schools and churches in residential areas. Use elevated points to pray over a panorama. Linger at specific sites which seem to be key.
4. **Pray with insight.** Pray for the people you see. As you do, you might find the Spirit of God recalibrating your heart with His own sensitivities. Enhance these responsive insights with research done beforehand. Use knowledge of past events and current trends to enrich intercession. Above all, pray Scripture. If you have no clear place to begin praying, select any of the biblical prayers, and you will find that they almost pray themselves.
5. **Focus on God.** Make God's promises rather than Satan's schemes the highlight of your prayer. Seek a restraining order from heaven upon evil so that God's empowered people may bring forth God's intended blessings on the city.
6. **Re-gather and report.** Share what you have experienced and prayed. Expressing something of your insights and faith will encourage others as well as yourself. Set plans for further prayerwalking.
7. **Coordinate efforts.** Enlist other praying people to join with friends to cover special areas. Give leadership by forming and mixing prayer bands. Seek to collect written notes recording which areas have been covered and what kinds of prayers have been prayed. Pool your insights to ascertain whether God is prompting a repeated focus on particular areas. Eventually aim to cover your entire town or city, unless God guides otherwise.

Creative things to Pray during a Prayerwalk

Keep prayers pertinent to the specific community you pass through. As you do, you will find prayers naturally progress to the nation and to the world.

Use a theme passage of Scripture. Unless God guides you to use another, try I Timothy 2:1-10. Many have found it to be a useful launching point for prayerwalking. Verse 8 speaks of the important territorial dimension to prayer connected with God's desire that all people be saved. "I want the men in every place to pray." Copy this and other passages in a format easy to read aloud several times during your walk. Each of the following prayer points emerges from this passage:

- Concerning Christ: Proclaim Him afresh to be the one Mediator and the ransom for all. Proclaim Him Lord of the neighborhood and of the lives you see.
- Concerning leaders: Pray for people responsible in any position of authority—for teachers, police, administrators and parents.
- Concerning peace: Cry out for the godliness and holiness of God's people to increase into substantial peace. Pray for new churches to be established.
- Concerning truth: Declare openly the bedrock reality that there is one God. Celebrate the faithful revelation of His truth to all peoples through ordinary people (I Timothy 2:8). Pray that the eyes of minds would cease to be blinded by Satan so that they could come to a knowledge of the truth.
- Concerning the blessing of God: Thanksgivings are to be made on behalf of all people. Give God the explicit thanks He deserves for the goodness He constantly bestows on the homes you pass by. Ask to see the city with His eyes, that you might sense what is good and pleasing in His sight as well as what things grieve Him deeply. Ask God to bring forth an enduring spiritual awakening.
- Concerning the church: Ask for healing in relationships, that there be no wrath or dissension among God's people. Ask that God would make His people, men and women alike, expressive in worship with the substance of radiant, relational holiness. Ask that our worship would be adorned with the confirming power of saints doing good in our communities.

Use your Eyes and Ears to Pray Creatively:

- Standing on a high place and seeing power lines between himself and the city below, you could pray that the Holy Spirit would empower those who ministered in that city.
- Waiting at a traffic light in a crowded city, you could pray with the changing of the lights that nonbelievers would exercise caution in their decisions, stop their sinful ways and go toward Jesus.
- Deafened by the noise of a city street, you could pray that those who live in that noisy city would be able to hear the still, small voice of God.
- Seeing a welder at his work, you could begin to sing, "It only takes a spark to get a fire going..." then pray for that spark.
- Hearing a siren, you could pray for safety until these people could hear and respond to the Gospel and also pray for those who offer physical and spiritual care in the city.
- Be creative...open your eyes, your ears and allow God to prompt you.

Sources: Adapted from articles found on www.peopleteams.org and www.dawneurope.net

Activity #4: Take a Walk (take 2)

30 minutes

Facilitator Instructions:
Instruct everyone that they have 10 minutes to go for a walk (a second time) in groups of 2-3. As they walk this time, encourage everyone to use some of the new ideas that they have been exposed to about prayerwalking.

Debrief:
Once everyone is gathered back together, spend some time debriefing the experience with the following question:

In what ways was this walk different than your first walk?

Reflections:

15-20
minutes

Activity #5: My Prayerwalking Game Plan

Facilitator Instructions:
As the final activity for this session, ask people to put together a prayerwalking plan that they will actually do for homework. Reinforce that their plan is something that they are to do in the next 30 days or before you meet the next time. If you have time, ask people to share their plans with a partner or two, and then pray for each other. If it is appropriate, this can also be a group brainstorming time if a group is going to do this as an activity together.

My Personal Prayerwalking Game Plan (a few planning questions)

Question #1: When will I prayerwalk?

Question #2: Who will I ask to join me in prayerwalking?

Question #3: Where will we prayerwalk?

Question #4: What are some specific issues and concerns I would like to pray for as I walk?

Question #5: What have I learned about prayerwalking that I want to remember or experiment with?

Helpful resources:
Hawthorne, Steve. *PrayerWalk Organizer Guide*. Prayer Walk USA, 1996.
Hawthorne, Steve. *Prompts for Prayerwalkers*. Waymakers.
Hawthorne, Steve & Graham Kendrick. *Prayerwalking*. Creation House, 1993.
www.peopleteams.org
www.waymakers.org
www.dawneurope.net

2 Community Surveying

How well do you know the city, town or local neighborhood in which your church sits? What are the needs that people face? What are the challenges? What areas of day-to-day life most need an experience with God?

Gathering information through surveys is one way to deepen your understanding of the community. The activities below provide options for doing so. The first activity is a simple way to talk as a group about the community. The second activity provides various ways for gathering information. And the third helps you make a plan.

Working through these activities will cause you to see your community from a new point of view. And for some, it will be like they are seeing it for the first time.

40 minutes

Activity #1: Reflecting on our Community

Part 1: At the beginning of the meeting, share what you have been learning and experimenting with since the group last met.

Part 2: Break the group into two teams. Each team has 20 minutes to discuss the questions below. One person should record the responses for their respective team. After the time is up, gather together and talk through each question. Consider recording the reflections on flipchart paper.

1. What are the unique needs where God has placed us? In our city? In our neighborhoods?

2. How are these needs reflected socially, economically, ethnically, environmentally, politically, and religiously?

3. What arena of our community is the farthest from God?

4. What special opportunities are found within our immediate (within ½ mile) sphere of influence?

5. What burning issues are alive in the public's eye and brought to attention by the media?

6. What needs and opportunities do the industries specific to our area create?

7. What is the most significant change in our community in the last decade and what need does this create?

8. What are the largest community events and what needs or opportunities do these create?

9. Because of our specific location, what solution could we provide that no other church could?

10. How would we describe the "atmosphere of lostness" in our community?

11. What is the history of our particular community and what insight does this provide?

12. Does the history of our community bring to light any spiritual strongholds?

13. What one positive change in our community would have the most dramatic effect to people's lives?

Questions adapted from Will Mancini, *Church Unique* (San Fransiscio: Jossey-Bass, 2008), 86-87.

30 minutes

Activity #2: Options for Knowing Your Community

Facilitator instructions:
The purpose of this block of time is to develop a strategy for getting out into the community. Have the group read the Knowing Your Community Surveying Tips below and then develop an action plan by asking the group to decide:

- Which survey assignments do we want to tackle?
- Who will take which assignments?
- When will the assignments need to be completed by?
- Decide on a date when you will reconvene to talk about what was discovered during the survey work done by the group.

Knowing Your Community Surveying Tips:
Natural Conversations—Look for opportunities. Being curious will open up rich opportunities.

Mapping—Place major landmarks, roads, barriers, and churches on a good map of the area. Analyze how the locations of these arteries and barriers could impact where your church is ministering. What trends and patterns are emerging to which you need to pay attention.

Demographic Study—Population shifts can be tricky to spot. In the next five years what will the makeup of your community look like? What age, ethnic, family, and socioeconomic changes are happening around you? Take advantage of any number of demographic surveying instruments that will provide a vast array of fresh insights about your area. Most denominational district offices provide free demographic information to member congregations. Link2Lead.com has excellent demographic information available at very reasonable introductory rates.

Community Leaders—One of the richest deposits of community insights can be gained from those who are serving the public. A thirty minute interview with a leader in your community will be eye-opening. Use the "Community Leader" survey below as an interview guide.

Another option is to invite as many community leaders as possible to participate in a focus group. This could be hosted at your church and the public could be invited to hear the leader's perspectives as well as ask their own questions. Be sure to provide snacks and drinks!

Consider making a visit to:
• Local government officials (Mayor, Aldermen, etc.)
• Planning and zoning office
• School board, teachers, and principals
• Community Service Agency (such as Child Protective Services)
• Police and Fire Stations
• Health Care professionals

Community Leader Interview Questions:
1. What are the greatest strengths of our community?
2. What would you like to see different in our community in 5 years, 10 or 15 years?
3. What are the three greatest challenges that may prevent these visions from developing?
4. What are the most pressing problems facing people living in our community?
5. How might we partner with you to improve our community?

Study the history—How did your city, town, or community come into existence? What caused people to move here? What have been the leading industries? How have the needs in the community changed in the last 5, 10, 25 years?

Other churches and religious organizations—What's going on spiritually in your community? How many cults and sects are present? Which churches are growing and why? What are these churches doing to connect with the community?

Identify sub-groups—As Ed Stetzer says, "The more you discover and learn about the people groups and community, the more effective you will become in relating to and communicating with all the people in your area. It is also likely that you will have many opportunities to minister to all kinds of people in your area." (*Breaking the Missional Code* p.223)

30 minutes

Activity #3: Planning a Community Survey

Facilitator instructions:
This is an additional way to find out more information about your community. It is also a great tool for getting more people involved in the process! Develop an action plan by asking the group to determine the following activities:

• Select the date for the survey.
• Recruit volunteers to conduct the survey.
• Identify the neighborhoods that will be surveyed (probably the same as the Prayerwalk).
• Meet at 10:00 am at the church on the Saturday selected, divide into pairs, assign neighborhoods to be surveyed, discuss the survey and how they need to conduct it by knocking on doors to ask the short questions and just gather information.
• This activity could also be done at a mall, park, or other public place where many people are gathered.

Community Survey Questions
Briefly identify and introduce yourself, saying "I'm a member of
_____ Church here in _____ and I'm doing a short three question survey. Do you have a minute to answer three questions?"

1. What three words would you use to describe _____ Church?
2. What needs do you see others in our community struggle with meeting?
3. If you were looking for a church home, what characteristics or qualities would you look for?

You can jot down a few notes on their answers, thank them, and if you feel comfortable, ask, "Would you have any needs or requests that we might pray for?" Then, just be on your way. Meet back at the church, at 11:30 am, to debrief, share stories and turn in your results.

Community Survey Planning Guide
Instructions: Use the worksheet below to list specific actions you intend to take related to each of the three Activities.

Specific Action Steps	Who is Responsible?	By When?

3 Visioning Day

Vision, Strategy, Plan, & Budget

This process can be compared to taking a trip. Before you leave, you have to choose the destination, i.e., the Vision. The better you describe the destination, the more enthusiasm you will generate among your travelling partners. To get to your destination, you need an idea of how you're going to get there (via car, train, or plane), i.e., the Strategy. The next thing to determine is the route. By what specific route will you arrive? This is the Plan. Finally, the mother of all questions: how much will the trip cost? This is the Budget.

All four questions must be answered and are necessary for dynamic change. The Vision question will be answered by the congregation, with the help of the staff. Once the Vision is determined, the staff team is then responsible for getting the church to its destination by answering the Strategy, Plan and Budget questions.

An Effective Vision Statement:
- Describes a preferred future
- Is Challenging yet Achievable: A "stretch" that can be accomplished
- Is Memorable: Keep it short, preferably less than one page
- Is Specific: Numbers, dates, and specific people groups are mentioned
- Is Emotive: Produces an emotional response. This must be done!

30 minutes

Step 1: Identify your Mission Target

In the movie *28 Days*, Sandra Bullock plays a character in a drug rehab program, where a professional baseball player is also a resident. One day, she finds him in the back woods of the center throwing baseballs at a mattress and comments that she could never hit the mattress. He replies that anyone could hit the mattress. She then throws a ball and misses. He says, "The problem is you're aiming at the mattress. Aim at the button in the middle of the mattress. If you aim at the button, you'll hit the mattress. If you aim at the mattress, you'll hit nothing." Of course, she then aims at the button and hits the mattress.

Visioning is about getting the congregation to aim at the button (a specific people group) knowing that in the process they'll most likely hit the mattress (the community). It is important to stress that this is a mission focus. This mission focus does not mean that other existing ministries will be eliminated. It does mean that the mission focus will have priority in budgeting of people, space, and dollars.

A. Review the Community Reflection Questions, the Community Leaders Interviews, and the Community Surveys that you have conducted, along with the Demographics you have compiled.
B. What stood out from these exercises? What surprised you? What bothers you about what you discovered?
C. Who are some of the most common unreached people groups in the survey area?
D. Display on screen the resulting composite.

Step 2: Understanding the Mission Target

30 minutes

A. What do they value? Where do they find community? What gives them joy?

B. What challenges do they face? What do they fear? Where are their hurts?

C. View Clip from the movie *Sister Act* and answer questions.
(The scene starts at 58:28 and ends at 1:03:15.)
Scene Set-up: Whoopi Goldberg plays a Las Vegas singer who is on the run from her gangster boyfriend. The police stash her away in a Catholic Convent where Whoopi has just been given the charge of developing the choir. Watch what happens in this interaction between the "street-smart" Whoopi and the ultra-conservative Reverend Mother.

Question #1: How would you describe the values of Whoopi, the Reverend Mother, and the Nuns?

Question #2: What dynamics did you notice unfolding in the scene as the nuns "took to the streets?" What did you observe as the nuns worked together?

Question #3: How are you personally challenged by what you saw in this scene?

D. Which of the 10 Most Receptive Groups are present in your Mission Field?

Top 10 Most Receptive Groups
- Church Visitors
- Friends of New Believers
- Recently Divorced Individuals
- First-time Parents
- Those with Marriage Problems
- Parents who are Experiencing Challenges
- Those Having Finanicial Struggles
- New Residents
- Those Facing Illness
- Those Recovering from Addiction

Group Activity:
In small groups, have each table write a short biographical narrative of a typical person in their assigned target group. Have them give their person a name, a face, and a story in which the congregation can sympathize. You can use the following as an example:

Ann is a 30-year-old married mother with a nine-year old-daughter, Jasmine, from a previous marriage. Ann was divorced when Jasmine was 18 months old and Ann remarried when Jasmine was four years old. Shortly after getting married she gave birth to a son, Troy. Ann and her husband, Chuck, both work low income jobs. Ann's salary barely covers day care. If costs continue to rise, Jasmine and Troy will have to become latchkey kids with the childcare responsibility falling upon Jasmine. Chuck and his step-daughter Jasmine have a strained relationship which causes tensions in he and Ann's marriage.

20 minutes

Step 3: Developing a Vision Strategy (What Must We Do to Reach Them?)

Discuss the following questions:

• What can we do to add value to their lives?

• What can we do to bring the power of God into their lives?

Step 4: Creating a compelling Vision Statement

30 minutes

(This step can be completed by the Pastor & Staff or the Pastor and a smaller group of leaders. Someone from the People of Passion Group should be included in the process if possible.)

A. Begin with an opening statement describing your mission target.
B. Include a statement describing why you desire to reach this target.
C. Include one or both of the following:
  • One or more statements that describe the general strategy
  • One or more statements that describe a plan for reaching the mission target

(Don't forget to include specific dates & numbers. These statements must be written in terms of what is seen & heard.)

Group Activity:
Have everyone put together a sample Vision Statement in small groups. Then have each group share their Vision Statement with the larger group. Evaluate each statement based on the four components above, as well as the criteria of an effective vision statement:

  • Describes a preferred future
  • Is Challenging yet Achievable: A "stretch" that can be accomplished
  • Is Memorable: Keep it short - less than one page in length
  • Is Specific: Numbers, dates, and specific people groups are mentioned
  • Is Emotive: Produces an emotional response. This must be done!

Example #1

Vision Statement	Statement Feature
We are a church that is fully committed to meeting the needs of kids and their families.	Mission Target
Our core value is children and we seek to reach our community through an on-site sports ministry which includes soccer, basketball, and softball seasons.	Strategy
We dream in the next five years of building an all-purpose sports complex that will allow us to expand our Just 4 Kids sports ministry.	Plan

Example #2

Vision Statement	Statement Feature
We dream of being a church where the poor and marginalized of our community are welcomed.	Mission Target
We are called to minister to those who have real needs through a food distribution system and a network of family support systems.	Strategy
We dream of being a church where real pain is ministered to through recovery, support groups and a full range of small groups.	Plan

Where do we go from here?
A. The pastor will begin to preach the Vision Statement.
B. The pastor will hone the Vision Statement into a powerful and memorable one.
C. The pastor, along with the staff and board, will develop a composite profile of the mission target.
D. Outreach events will be tailored to attract the models described.
E. Success of outreach events will be measured with the question, "Did our mission target show up?"

4 Service Projects

There is church stuff. And then there is the rest of life. For many, they don't see how the two overlap. What God does in the church has little to do with day-to-day life. So the only option is to try and get people to come to church services and events.

As good as our church services might be, God's people have to find a way to engage people in the normal stuff of life. God is at work all around, and we need practical ways to demonstrate God's love beyond the walls of the church.

These activities are experimental ways of demonstrating God's tangible love for people in the here and now. If you have never done anything like this before, remember you are experimenting. You might be shocked at the impact such acts of kindness will have on others ... and on you.

20 minutes

Activity One: Discussion of Article

Facilitator instructions:
Give the small group an opportunity to read the short article on the next page. Then discuss:

Question #1: What gets in the way of you performing acts of kindness?

Question #2: In what way are you personally challenged by what you just read?

Improving Your Serve Article

In the book, *Irresistible Evangelism*, a working definition of kindness is suggested as "demonstrating God's love by offering to do humble acts of service, in Christ's name, with no strings attached." The authors go on to say,

"We'll never shine brightly in the kingdom of God until we can sign up for activities that bring us no immediate, tangible, specific gain. We need to learn the lesson Jesus taught in Luke 6:35 about giving without expecting to get anything back, not even gratitude. The only reward we need is knowing that we're acting like sons of the Most High. The watching world will never be genuinely interested in our message as long as we come across as self-seeking promoters of our little piece of the kingdom. However, the world hungers for generosity in Christ's name when those expressing it don't care who gets the credit. If we don't take seriously the phrases In Christ's name and with no strings attached, we're just using a manipulative marketing strategy."

When we serve another, with no strings attached, we are operating in a way that is counter-cultural. Doing something for nothing is unheard of these days. A posture of a servant can easily be drown out by the "me, my, and mine" slogans of Madison Avenue. But let's remember…it is the kindness of God that has drawn us into a saving relationship. Through His kindness, God has rescued us from the kingdom of darkness and pulled us out of the miry clay. Through His many acts of kindness in the New Testament, Jesus gives us a model of what it means to be kind. Steve Sjogren, one of the co-authors of *Irresistible Evangelism*, shares a powerful personal story about acts of kindness. He was in the midst of recovering from a life threatening surgery-gone-bad. While he was in the hospital he shares:

"I was at the lowest point of my life in every way-physically, emotionally, and spiritually; I desperately needed to give something away to get better. All I could think of that was available to me was popsicles. So whenever visitors asked if there was anything they could do for me, I didn't even let them finish the sentence.

'Have you got any pocket change?' I would ask.

If they did, I'd have them roll me in my wheelchair down the hallway to the Popsicle machine. They would spring for a lap-full of the tasty treats, and then we would go up and down the hallways looking for patients to give them to. The only guideline: Only patients not on ventilators could get a Popsicle!"

Source: Steve Sjogren, Dave Ping, and Doug Pollock, *Irresistible Evangelism* (Loveland, CO: Group Publishing, 2003).

Activity Two: Selecting a Service Project

Facilitator Instructions:

Give the small group time to reflect on the Service Project Ideas listed on the following pages. Encourage people to mark ideas that intrigue them or interest them as possible ideas for the small group to do together.

Use a whiteboard or a flipchart to begin brainstorming a list of up to 10 ideas that the group would like to consider.

Narrow the discussion down to the "one idea" that group will tackle in the next couple of weeks.

Form a simple plan for the service project by agreeing on:

1. What we will do?

2. When will we do the project?

3. Where will we do the project?

4. How will we do the project?

5. Who will take responsibility for the various tasks?

6. Are there other people or groups we can enlist to help?

Service Project Ideas

Public Places
Soft Drink Giveaways
Newspapers
Vinyl Gloves
Umbrella Escorts
Windshield Washing
Coffee Giveaways
Restroom Cleaning
Urinal Screens
Restroom Deodorizer
Grocery Bag Loading Assistance
Bag Packing at Self-Serve
Grocers
Grocery Cart Returns
Quarters Attached to Cards for
  Phone Calls or Parking Meters
Donut Giveaway during Morning
  Traffic
Cookies
Lifesavers
Dollar Drop
Quarter Drop
Chewing Gum
Lollipops / Blow Pops
Small Bags of Taffy
Gourmet Chocolates (Truffles)
Bottled Water Giveaway
Flower Seeds
Freshen-up Packs - (mints &
  moist towelettes)

Sporting Events
Coffee Giveaways
Soft Drink Giveaways
Popcorn
Popsicles
Windshield Washing
Peanuts
Sunglasses (cheap ones!)
Hand Cleaning Towelettes
Freshen-up packs - (mints &
  moist towelettes)
Trash Pick Up
Bottled Water Giveaway
Glow in the Dark Necklaces

Downtown
Windshield Washing
Soft Drinks for Shoppers
Parking Meter Feeding
Umbrella Escorts
Business Window Washing

Toilet Cleaning
Cart Token for Shopping Carts
Employee Soft Drink Giveaway
Cookies
Cappuccino
Polaroids at Carriage Rides
Shoe Shines
Hand Cleaning Towelettes
Stamps in Front of Post Office
Seeds on Cars

Parks
Doggie Treats
Pet Festivals
Hot Dog Grilling
Helium Balloons for Kids
Polaroid Family Photos
Picnic
Ice Cream Coupons
Gatorade at Biking Trails
Pictionary in the Park
Flower Seed Packets
Face Painting
Doggie Dirt Cleanup
Doggie Wash
Golf Balls
Golf Tees
Golf Ball Cleaning
Pump-up Spray Water Bottles
Clowning
Bottled Water Giveaway

Automobiles
Car Wash
Windshield Washing
Check Oil and Fill
Single Mom's Oil Change
Washer Fluid Fill
Tire Pressure Check
Interior Vacuuming
Interior Window Cleaning
Bulb Replacement
Windshield Ice Scraping at
  Apartment Complexes
Windshield Ice Scrapers
Freeing Cars Stuck in the Snow
Car Drying at Car Washes
Windshield Washing at Self-
  Serve Gas Stations
Buy Down Gas to Bargain Price
Hand Cleaning Towelettes at
  Gas Pumps

Roadsides & Traffic Lights
Parking Meter Feeding
Summer Car Washes
Coke Giveaways
Winter Car Washes/ Desalting
Popsicle Giveaways
Trash Pickup with "Kindness in
  Progress" Signs
Towelettes Giveaway on Side of
  the Road

College Campuses
Bike Fix-up
Pen and Pencil Giveaways
Post Cards and Stamps
Photocopying
Floppy Discs
Tutoring
Soft Drinks, Gatorade, and
  Lemonade at Class Sign-up
Dorm Room Cleaning
Drinks at Intramural Athletics
Drinks at Greek Events
Breakfast Pop Tarts
Test Essay Booklets
Exam Answer Sheets
Coffee and Tea during Late Night
  Study Sessions
Pizza on Move-In Day at Dorms
Quarter Drop
Long Distance Phone Cards
Ice Cream Coupons
Care Packages for Students
Gum, Blow Pops
Snacks (chips, crackers)

Malls & Shopping Centers
Christmas Gift Wrapping
Dollar Drop
Meal Purchasing at Food Court
Quarters in Coin Returns
Long Distance Phone Cards
Ice Cream Cone Coupons
Package Check-In
Childcare during Christmas
  Shopping
Coffee/Hot Chocolate Coupons

Holidays

Chocolate Hearts on Valentine's
Roses on Valentine's
Green Foiled Coins at St. Patrick's Day Parades
Easter Baskets for Businesses
Butterfly Cocoons for Easter
Easter Candy Giveaway
Flower Seeds for Spring
Mother's / Father's Day Carnation Giveaways
Independence Day Festival Glow in the Dark Necklaces
July 4th Picnics House to House
Independence Day Festival Giveaways: Blow Pops, Gum
Labor Day - School Supplies
Halloween - Reverse Trick or Treat (House to House to give them candy)
Thanksgiving - Door to Door Turkey
Door to Door Mums
Fall Candy Giveaway
Fall Leaf Raking
Christmas: Gift Wrap at Mall
Christmas: Giveaway Special
Caroling and Candy Canes
Door to Door Poinsettias
Scotch Tape Giveaway
Christmas Tree Giveaway
Snow Shoveling
Winter Survival Kit

High School & College Sports

Oranges for Football Practice
High School Sports Party
Watermelon after practice
Gatorade after a hard practice
Facilitate a community service project
Make hospital visits
Greet students and parents and help the freshmen move in
Baby-sit for the coaches
Physical therapy rehab
Care packages for finals week
Offer tutoring
Honor a team at your athletic meeting
Shovel manure
Go to lesser followed sports
Set up social settings
Make own Appreciation Day

Capture seasonal times with high touch ideas
Take a camera to practice/games
Clean up after a sporting event
Meet with freshmen for a coke
Organize surprise mini-birthday parties
Give away peanuts/popcorn at sporting events
Offer to do videoing of a practice
Offer to keep stats
Free car washes for the athletic department

House to House

Fruit Giveaway
Sunday Morning Paper and Coffee Giveaways
Leaf Raking
Lawn Mowing
Grass Edging
Screen Cleaning
Rain Gutter Cleaning
Garbage Can Return from Curb
Food Delivery to Shut-Ins
Kitchen Cleanup
General Yard Cleanup
Door to Door Carnation
Tulip Bulbs
Potted Plant Giveaways
Flower Seed Packet Giveaways
Sidewalk Sweeping
Windshield Washing
Snow Removal from Walks and Drives
Window Washing
Minor House Repairs
General Interior Cleaning
Community Dinner
Doggie Yard Cleanup
Weed Spraying
Tree Limb Trimming
Light Bulb Replacement
Seal Blacktop Driveways
Fireplace Ash Removal
Radon Detectors
Carbon Monoxide Detectors
Smoke Detector Batteries
Fragrance Spraying
Dog Washing
Filter Change for AC / Heater
Garage Cleaning
Fireplace Kindling
Bark and Mulch for Yards

Salt for Snowy Driveways
House Number Painting on Curbs
Shopping Assistance for Shut-ins
Poinsettias at Christmas
Picnics at Independence Day
Easter Baskets

Miscellaneous

Steaks & Salmon for Firefighters
Gasoline for Your Neighbor
Cleaning Up at Food Courts
Toilet Seat Covers
Birthday Party Organizing
Pay Library Fines
Winter Survival Kit
Suntan Lotion
Surf Wax
Summer Survival Kit
"Biggie Size" Food Orders in Fast Food Drive Thru Lanes
Blood Pressure Screening
Mother's Day Carnation
Car Drying at Self-Serve Car Washes
Grocery Store Bag Packing
Free Bird Feeders and Refills to Convalescent Home Residents
Christmas Tree Collection
Christmas Tree Giveaway
Bait at Local Fishing Spots
Coffee at Bus or Subway Stops
Pay Laundromat Washer & Dryer
Memorial Service for Unchurched
Carnations to Cemetery Visitors
Easter Baskets
Pizza on Moving Day at Apartments
Move In Welcoming Party
Lawn Mower Tune-up
Time Change Reminder Flyer
Cocoons on Good Friday
Church Match Books
Scotch Tape at Christmas

List Adapted from: http://www.servantevangelism.com

5 Crafting a Personal Testimony

Every Christian has a story. You have a story. However, do you know how to share it with others? Do you know how to share it in a way that others will want to hear it? Do you know how to share it in a way that points to what Jesus has done in your life?

Honestly, it's not difficult to tell your story with impact. You don't have to be a great speaker or have a dramatic conversion experience. You just need to know what to highlight and practice it a bit.

The following activities walk you through the steps of sharing your testimony. At first, it might feel wooden and rough. But that's normal. The more you rehearse it, the more natural it will become. Your story is of high value because God has changed you. It's one worth telling and there are people who need to hear it. Preparing yourself for those people is what these activities are all about.

20 minutes **Activity 1: The Power of Stories**

Facilitator instructions:
Take a few minutes as a group and reflect on the following question together:

> "What are some of the reasons that we like to share and listen to stories? In other words, what makes stories so powerful?"

• Things to consider
- How do stories touch our emotions?

- How do stories help us connect with another person?

- How does our personal experience make our stories credible?

Activity 2: "Crafting Your Personal Testimony"

1. Read this introduction together.
   God has done some very unique things in our lives. Some very powerful stories reside in each one of us. Our story with God can and needs to be shared with those who need God's grace in Jesus Christ. One of the most effective ways of sharing our faith is by telling a story about our own journey with God. Remember, stories are powerful! Today, let's take a look at the steps involved in writing your own personal story...your personal testimony.

2. As a group, talk through the five steps of writing your own story. (See pages 43-47.)

3. After the brief overview, invite someone from the group to share their story. This person should be chosen in advance (before the group meets) and asked to prepare their story according to the five steps. While sharing, everyone else should listen for the various "writing your story steps." You are shooting for a story that can be completed in under five minutes.

4. Spend a little time debriefing together as a group. Identify the steps together. Ask the group if they have any suggestions for ways that the person could polish their story.

5. Now turn everyone loose to work on their own story. Let them know that they have 10-15 minutes to work on their draft.

   For those who have been Christians from early childhood, focus your story on a time when God intervened in your life. Find a 'grace story' that a non-believer would hear and find hope in God and His grace.

6. After everyone has worked on their draft, have them get into pairs or triads depending on how much time you have available. Triads will take a little bit longer but is a better experience overall. Give each person five minutes to share their story with their partner(s). Ask the listeners to give two minutes of feedback on their story...
   -what went well?
   -was anything unclear? Are there any ways to polish their story for more impact?

7. Close out the session back in pairs/triads. Have everyone share the name of a presumably non-Christian that they would like to share their story with in the next week (or your own predetermined period of time). Encourage people to create the opportunity by saying something like this: "I'm taking a class (or course) at my church and one of my assignments this week is to share a story with a friend about my life with God. Would you mind if I grabbed 10 minutes (now) or sometime this week to tell you a little bit about my life? I promise...no strings attached or Bible thumping!"

Commitment to share your story. End with prayer in the sharing pairs or triads. Pray by name for those to whom you will be speaking.

5 steps to Crafting a Personal Testimony

Step #1 Identify life and heart themes
Step #2 What my life was like distant from Christ.
Step #3 How I came to realize that I needed Christ.
Step #4 How I was drawn near to Christ.
Step #5 The difference Jesus has made in my life.

Step #1: Looking at the list below of life and heart themes, check the boxes that were present in your life before your relationship with God became meaningful. This list is provided to get you thinking about your life before meeting God.

Life and Heart Themes

❑ Worries/Anxiety............................ Inner Peace
❑ Guilt/Shame............................... Forgiveness
❑ Anger/Temper............................. Patience and love
❑ Emptiness/Lack of Purpose.............. Purpose in life
❑ Grief....................................... Comfort and joy
❑ Stress/Burnout............................ Power for living
❑ Low self-esteem.......................... Significance to God
❑ Poor health............................... Strength to go on
❑ Disappointment.......................... Trust in his good plans
❑ Insecurity................................. Confidence and security
❑ Regrets.................................... A second chance at life
❑ Discontent-Always busy.................. Contentment and peace
❑ Fears...................................... Faith to face my fears
❑ Loneliness................................ He's always with me
❑ Addictions/Habits........................ Power to change
❑ Self-centeredness........................ Love for other people
❑ Despair/Depression....................... Hope
❑ Cheap thrills.............................. Real, lasting happiness
❑ Boredom with my life..................... Adventure with God
❑ Fear of Death............................. Assurance of heaven
❑ "Something was missing"................. Sense of fulfillment
❑ Bitterness & Resentment.................. Freedom from my past
❑ Pain of rejection.......................... God's unconditional love
❑ Marriage Problems........................ Changes in my marriage
❑ Financial Problems........................ Changes in my finances
❑ Business Problems........................ Changes in my business

Step #2: What my life was like distant from Christ.*
- What common circumstances would an unbeliever identify with?
- What were your attitudes that an unbeliever would identify with?
- What was most important to you then?
- What substitute for God did you use to find meaning in your life? (sports/ fitness, success at work, marriage, sex, making money, drugs/alcohol, having fun, entertainment, popularity, hobbies, other)

*If you've been a believer since early childhood, then reflect on this question:
- "What are some difficulties or challenges that God has helped you face that could serve as a connecting point, as a window of grace, with a non-believer?"

Step #3: How I came to realize that I needed Christ.
- What significant steps led up to your conversion?
- What needs, hurts, or problems added to your realization that you needed Jesus?
- How did God get your attention?
- What motivated you or made the difference at that time?

Step #4: How I was drawn near to Christ.
- What specifically happened that drew you to Jesus?
- Where did it happen?
- Who did God use to bring you to Jesus?
- What Bible passage was especially meaningful to you at that time?

Step #5: The difference Jesus has made in my life.
- What blessings have you experienced or felt?
- What problems have been resolved?
- How has Jesus helped you change for the better?
- How has it helped your relationships? Give a current example.

Use this page and the next to write out your testimony.

6 Outreach Events

Outreach events provide great opportunities for people to gain exposure to the message of God's love as well as build relationships with Christians who take the Word of God seriously. Research has shown that most people become followers of Jesus after many exposures to the message and generally in the context of a relationship with a believer. The common notion that people become believers in Jesus after one opportunity to hear the Gospel is not accurate.

We need to demonstrate the love of God in practical ways so that people outside the church can see what it means to follow Jesus. There are literally thousands of ways to do this, and it works best when it is done in ways that fit your local context. You cannot transport something that works in one church and expect it to work in exactly the same way in yours. Think and pray together about what might work best for the people who live near you.

The activities below are designed to walk you through practical steps to develop an outreach event that will work for you. Put a plan together. Work the plan. Then review what you did. God will open your eyes in the process.

Activity: Building a Great Outreach Event

Here are four steps for developing an outreach event that will have an impact and touch people's lives:

1. As a group, read the "7 Questions for Building a Great Outreach Event" article (see page 49).

2. Discuss some of the ideas in the 7 Questions by suggesting ideas for running a successful event at your church.

3. As a group, take time to carefully consider the various outreach event ideas listed on page 50. Brainstorm other ideas that could work and then narrow the best ideas down to the one idea that the small group is most excited about.

4. Using Post-it® notes in the form of the chart on page 55, start building an outreach event plan. Decide on the next planning meeting you will have and hand out assignments to the group that need to be followed up on before you end the meeting.

7 Questions for Building a Great Outreach Event

1. WHEN will you run your event?
Consider the time of the year when planning the outreach/harvest event. For instance, when hunting season is complete would be a great time to have a Wild Game Supper for all the hunters and hunter want-to-be's. The Super Bowl is the first Sunday in February. This is a great time to have a Super Bowl Party. March is a great time to have a Spring Fling at the city park. TIMING is everything.

2. WHO do you hope will come?
Who needs to be reached at this event? When this is answered, the event can be tailor made for this specific target audience. Men, women, youth, children, singles, senior adults, etc. are all possible targets.

3. How much will it COST?
To have a successful outreach event, there must be some of God's money involved. Ask God to provide a plan that will reach many for Christ and then trust him to provide for his plan. When it comes to reaching people for Christ, Christ will always provide. Encourage people to give toward the event. Make it a first class event.

4. What's the PLAN for the event?
To have a successful outreach event, preparation must take place before the event.

5. Who can help as a VOLUNTEER?
Any successful event rises and falls on the ability of the leadership to accomplish the task. In recruitment, involve an entire cross section of the church. Involve children, youth, adults, singles and senior adults so the entire church can feel ownership of the event.

6. How will we PROMOTE the event?
Position every church member to be a promoter of the event. Provide posters or promotional material (done well) and encourage members to use these tools to invite their friends, family and co-workers. PUBLICIZE 4-6 six weeks out with posters and then do a heavy push 7-10 days before.

7. What is your plan for PRAYER?
Pray that all in the church will participate with joy and unity of heart. Pray that many lost and unchurched in the community will attend the outreach event. Enlist prayer teams and other groups to join you in praying for the event.

Outreach Ideas

- Carnivals (e.g. moon bounces, kids programming, etc.)
- Co-sponsor large community events (partnering with local communities and civic organizations)
- Free skating party
- Super Bowl Party
- Celebrity Golf Tournament
- Public servant recognition day (for police, fire fighters, etc.)
- Free movie night
- Free concerts (series of summer evening concerts)
- Vacation Bible School (or Backyard Vacation Bible School in numerous homes)
- Neighborhood cookouts and pool parties
- Community/neighborhood block parties
- Family movie nights (free movies with popcorn and drinks)
- Sporting tournaments (e.g. 3 on 3 basketball tournament, flag football league, etc.)
- Sponsor classic car show
- Special Christmas Eve service
- Community New Year's Eve party
- July 4th
- Valentine's Day Dinner
- Family Fun Day
- Halloween/Harvest Carnival
- Parent's night outs (fun activities for kids at church while parents go out)

Other ideas:

-

-

-

-

Outreach Event Planner

Instructions:
Reproduce the chart below and brainstorm action steps that you will need to work through to plan an Outreach Event. Use the questions below to stimulate your thinking. One action step goes on one Post-it® note. Don't worry about sequencing the Post-it® notes initially. You can do that after you have brainstormed your action steps.

Next Step Questions:
- Who should be included in this?
- When can we get started?
- What needs to be sorted out first?
- How will we get started?
- How should we promote this?
- What decisions need to get made?
- When will we review our progress?
- Other Actions? _____

30-Day Action Steps	60-Day Action Steps	90-Day Action Steps

Place Post-it Notes on the Next Steps Chart

7 Talking About the Gospel

Sharing the Gospel presentation with those who do not know Christ is crucial. But often we find ourselves intimidated by the idea. Our overwhelming tendency is to shift the burden of sharing the Gospel to our professional workers who have the training. However, by far, most people are introduced to Christ through a friend, neighbor, relative or co-worker. You have people in your life who may be poised to hear the message of the Gospel from you, but not from a pastor.

This exercise equips you to share the Gospel in a conversational, informal way. This is not about preaching or memorizing a canned message. It's a way to introduce what God has done through Jesus and invite people to talk through it with you.

The way to get comfortable in doing it is to practice it. The information itself you may have heard 500 times. However, we need to develop the skills that will enable us to have graceful conversations around the Gospel. Get ready for the doors God will open when you do.

Activity 1: Simple Gospel Sharing

One person should talk through the parts of the Gospel presentation that is outlined below (See pages 57-63). Draw the bridge illustration on a white board or a flipchart. Another person can play the role of the non-Christian. Ask the participants to build the illustration with you and remind them that you will be giving them a chance to draw it for someone else after you are done.

Only one passage is used in this method: Romans 6:23.

The key to this method is to engage people in a conversation that encourages them to share their life's situation and their personal application of the truths of this Bible verse to their own life. The best way to engage them in the conversation is to ask them questions. As you are unpacking the verse, circle the different key words.

Activity #2: Practice

Get into groups of three to practice the bridge illustration. Each person will need a fresh piece of paper to draw the bridge illustration out. Each triad will have one person drawing, one person role playing the "lost person" and another person as the observer. After each presentation, allow for a short time of feedback and then rotate the presenter role, the observer role, and the non-Christian role.

Each presenter will have 5-7 minutes to work through the entire bridge illustration. Use Bibles to explain the bridge illustration if you feel comfortable. However, the use of one verse should give you the focus needed to stay on track.

After each person is finished presenting, the other two people should give them feedback on how the presentation went. Ask them to give feedback around these two questions:
> Question #1: What went well in the presentation?
> Question #2: In what ways can the presentation be polished?

Debrief
Stay in triads. Ask for feedback on the practice session.
> -What was it like for you personally?
> -What went well?
> -What was difficult or frustrating?

Practice Again
When learning a gospel presentation like this, some get the impression that they are learning it in order to "lay it on someone." This is not a canned sales pitch. When practicing this presentation, it is helpful to do it a second time, but in a more conversational way. The one playing the role of the non-Christian would ask conversational questions and the "presenter" would have to respond in conversational ways. This "second round" of presenting will require more than 5-7 minutes.

Activity #3: Implementation

In triads, everyone should name a non-Christian that they would like to share the bridge illustration with during the next week (or your own pre-determined period of time). Take time in your triad to ask each member how they plan to invite their friend to meet with them. (Emphasize the need to be up front and straight-forward). One way of creating such an opportunity is to say something like this: "In a class I'm taking at my church, I was taught an illustration that connects God with our personal lives that really made sense to me. As an assignment, we were asked to share this illustration with a friend and I thought of you. Would you mind if we got together for a half an hour or so this week to share the illustration and talk about it? I promise . . . no strings attached (or something to that effect). I just want to share it and get your thoughts on it."

What's the point of "practicing" with a non-Christian? The point of sharing the illustration with a non-Christian is to engage them in meaningful conversation around the key concepts of the illustration. That will require 1) Sharing a concept, 2) Talking briefly about your understanding of it, 3) Asking the non-Christian to reflect on the concept (What do they think?), and 4) Listening to what they say and responding honestly to their thoughts as you proceed to the next concept in the illustration.

Commit to share the bridge with one person in the next week. Close out the time by praying in triads:
> -pray by name for openness of the non-Christians
> -pray for boldness and courage to share
> -pray for clear communication of Romans 6:23 and the bridge
> illustration.

The Gospel Presentation

Step 1:WAGES

Open your Bible to Romans 6:23 and ask the person to read the verse aloud to you while you write it at the top of a piece of paper.

Draw a box around the word "WAGES", then write it midway down the left side of the page and box it there also.

"How would you define the term wages?" (Wages are the reward we receive for what we have done. They are something that we have actually earned.)

"How might a person feel if his or her boss refused to pay them the wages that they were due? How would you feel? Deep down, we all know that it is only right that people get what they have earned. We earn wages from God for how we have lived our lives."

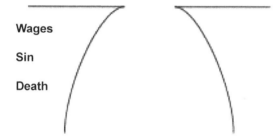

For the wages of sin is death
but the gift of God is eternal life
in Christ Jesus our Lord.

Wages

Sin

Death

Step 2: SIN

Draw a box around "SIN" in the verse and then write it below "WAGES." Draw a box around it there.

"What do you think of when you hear the word sin?"

"What would be your idea of a person who was perfect, who never sinned?" Do you know anyone, including you or me, who can honestly say that they have not sinned? (This should help them see that even by their own definition they fall short of living a good and perfect life.)

"Sin is more an attitude than an action—it can be a hostile or apathetic response to God and the standards that He gave us to live by. At any time in your life, has God seemed far away?" (Their answer deserves to be explored to the depth that they feel comfortable. If they answer "yes" you might ask, "How so?" If they do not want to talk about it, then go forward. The point is that they are actually thinking about being separated from God.)

If they answer "yes," draw in the lines of the cliff on both sides and explain that sin has separated everyone from God.

(If they are struggling with the idea of "sin separating us from God" you might use the following illustration or one that suits them better: "Imagine that you agreed with your teenager on rules regarding how to use your computer. What would happen if she ignored the rules and ruined your computer? Would that create a separation or problem in your relationship? Our sin creates a distance between us and God.")

Step 3: DEATH
Draw a box around the word "DEATH," write it down on the illustration, and box it there.

"What thoughts come to mind when you think of death?" (Have them answer the question. They may talk about physical death—maybe even going to heaven or hell. They may also think of death in other ways, such as the death of a relationship, or death of trust, or a life's dream. All of these answers are included in what the Bible calls "death".)

"Death often means separation—in the most obvious understanding, when we die our soul is separated from our body. If a person has lived their life here on earth separated from God, that separation will continue into eternity: the separation will ultimately result in eternal separation from God and everyone and everything that we care about. That would be a living hell. Not only will he experience separation from God today, but also forever."

"The reality of death is something that we also face before we actually die. Marriages end or families are torn apart—that's a death." We lose our trust in others when they hurt us or betray us. Or someone has deeply hurt us or taken something from us that can never be gotten back. Or we have made a wreck of our life's plans or dreams by some mistake or bad decision that we made. All of these are part of what this Bible verse means by the word "death."

Step 4: BUT

Draw a box around "BUT" in the verse and write it in a box between the bases of the cliffs.

"This is the most important word in the verse because it indicates that there is hope for all of us. What we have talked about so far is bad news, but God has good news. What we're going to talk about now is a contrast to what we just discussed."

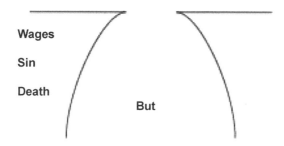

Step 5: GIFT

Draw a box around "GIFT" in the verse and write it on the right side of the cliff. Box it there.

"What is the difference between a gift and wages?"

(From now on, be sure to point back and forth to each side of the cliff to emphasize that the words contrast with each other.)

"A gift is not earned by the person who receives it, but someone else pays for it and gives it to you freely, hopefully, with no strings attached. How do you feel towards someone who gives you an expensive gift?"

"Some people try to bridge the separation they feel with God by trying to earn God's favor by doing good deeds, living moral lives, or taking part in religious activities. But it is impossible to bridge the separation ourselves if it has already been done by someone else. Just like it is impossible to earn something that has already been bought."

"Say you wanted to buy a special gift for a close friend to show how much that person means to you. How would you feel if the friend refused to accept it without first paying you for it?"

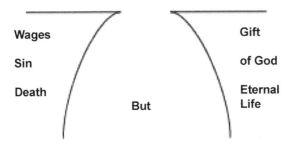

For the wages of sin is death
but the gift of God is eternal life
in Christ Jesus our Lord.

Wages

Sin

Death

But

Gift

of God

Eternal
Life

Step 6: OF GOD

Draw a box around "OF GOD" and write it on the right side of the cliff, across from "SIN." Box it.

Point to "SIN" on the left side and then back to "GOD" on the right and explain that all of us have sinned but God is perfect and has not.

"God has a gift for you and wants with all of his heart that you have it. I can't give it to you; a church can't give it to you; no one can give you this gift but God alone. Why do you think God would want to give you a gift? Why does anyone want to give someone a precious gift?"

Step 7: ETERNAL LIFE

Draw a box around "ETERNAL LIFE" and write it on the right side of the cliff with a box around it.

"What do you think eternal life is?" (Have them answer the question. They may talk about living forever or going to heaven or something like being reincarnated . It may not be the best time to argue about whether we go to heaven or come back to earth as something or someone else. The key here is that people generally tend to see human life as something that should not end.)

Point to "DEATH" on the left side and show that "ETERNAL LIFE" is the opposite. "Eternal life means a relationship with God in blissful harmony forever. Just as separation from God starts in this life and extends into eternity, eternal life starts now and goes on forever. No sin can end it. This "eternal life" includes a restored relationship with God, restored purpose in our selves, and often restored relationships with those we love. It's actually our lives as God intended them to be when he first gave them to us, before sin messed them up."

(Ask if there is any part that you have explained so far that he does not understand or if he has any questions. Be sure that each point is clear before you proceed any further. If necessary, go back and explain each point that is not clear.)

Step 8: CHRIST JESUS
Draw a cross between the cliffs as a bridge. Box the words "CHRIST JESUS" in the verse. Write "CHRIST JESUS" inside the cross.

"Jesus is the means by which God bridges the separation between himself and us. We are not able to find our way over to God, so God chose to find his way over to us. He did that by sending his own Son to us, Jesus. It is through Jesus that God gives us eternal life. No one can offer a gift except the one who purchased it. Jesus purchased our new life by paying for it with His own life. Jesus is the only person who ever lived a perfect life, no sin. He was never separated from God, His Father. They were always one in heart, mind, and love. To bridge the separation between God and ourselves, the wedge that our sins created needed to be taken away and the gap closed. God did that by taking our sins from us and placing them onto his perfect Son. While Jesus was dying on the cross, he actually became separated from his Father. Our sins, now on him, did that. His death bridged our separation from God. God completely removed our sins from us, thus closing the gap that stood between us and him. Jesus' death on the cross was the payment that God made to purchase the gift of eternal life that he so wants us to enjoy. The proof that Jesus' "payment" was sufficient to remove our sins and death is fact that Jesus rose from the dead. Death could not keep him locked up. Eternal death is just like a debtor's prison. We stay in prison until our debt is paid in full. Jesus paid our sins' debt in full, and so death had to set him (and us) free."

"Imagine that a police officer writes you a ticket for speeding and you go to court and the judge finds you guilty. But to your surprise, the policeman pays your fine out of his own pocket. Once paid, we are free to go. In the same way, Jesus paid the fine for you—death."

Or use this illustration. "A person is dying because his heart is diseased. Someone volunteers to donate his heart for a transplant, knowing that he will have to die in order to give it up. That would be the ultimate gift that one person could give to another. That is what Jesus gave to each of us personally."

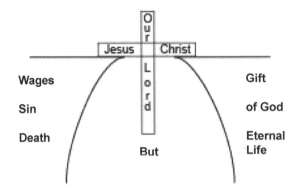

For the wages of sin is death
but the gift of God is eternal life
in Christ Jesus our Lord.

Step 9: OUR LORD

Box "OUR" and "LORD" in the verse, and write it inside the cross on the illustration. "The word 'our' means that something belongs to both of us, like, 'That is our car.' It is a word that indicates together, not separation. When this Bible verse says that Jesus Christ is now "our" Lord, it means that we are no longer separated from him. We are finally together again."

Lord refers to someone who has ultimate authority. When he or she says something, or gives an order, it happens. He has the final say in the matter. Jesus told the religious leaders of his day that he had "authority to forgive sins." That is, he had the authority to take our sins away so that they no longer control our lives and keep us separated from God. Do you want Jesus to take your sins away so that you are no longer separated from God? If you are answering yes, then know for a fact that Jesus is your Lord and that he has already taken your sins away from you. You are no longer separated from God. You will never receive the wages for your sin that we talked about earlier.

If you believe that Jesus died for you and rose from the dead, then you have received the gift of eternal life that he purchased for you. Do you believe that Jesus died and rose again for your forgiveness and salvation? If the answer is "yes," then I can assure you that "This is a miracle that God worked within you as you have just confessed your faith in Him! The Bible says, 'If you confess with your mouth that Jesus is Lord and believe in your heart that God raised him from the dead, you will be saved. . . For everyone who believes in him will not be put to shame.'"

Summary

For the wages of sin is death
but the gift of God is eternal life
in Christ Jesus our Lord.

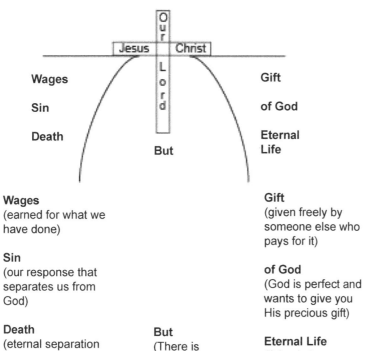

Wages
(earned for what we
have done)

Sin
(our response that
separates us from
God)

Death
(eternal separation
from God)

But
(There is
hope, Good
News!)

Gift
(given freely by
someone else who
pays for it)

of God
(God is perfect and
wants to give you
His precious gift)

Eternal Life
(living in harmony
with God forever)

Christ Jesus our Lord

Jesus bridges the gap between
God and man as he becomes our
substitute.
Faith in Jesus assures us of
eternal life.

Gospel presentation adapted from material that Randy Raysbrook developed on:
http://philnavs.org/site/literature/illustrations/oneverseevangelism/

CPSIA information can be obtained at www.ICGtesting.com
Printed in the USA
LVOW011107160812

294532LV00005B/5/P